Angel Readings

for Beginners

Elizabeth J. Foley

Unveil the mystery and master the technique
of angel readings. Learn how to conduct
an angel reading using oracle cards.

Published and distributed in the United States by Angel Street Publishing, LLC, P.O. Box 7298, Nashua, NH 03060 ♥ www.angelstreetpublishing.net.

Book design: Robin Wrighton, IDT Design, P.O. Box 622 Winchester, MA 01890

Printed by: King Printing Company, Inc. ♥ www.kingprinting.com

Angel Readings for Beginners / Elizabeth J. Foley

ISBN 10: 0-9800806-2-2
ISBN 13: 978-0-9800806-2-9

September 2008

Printed in the United States of America

CONTENTS

1

CHAPTER

INTRODUCTION TO THE ANGELIC REALM

What Are Angels

Every person regardless of age, race, gender or religious background has guardian angels. Your guardian angels were assigned to you before you incarnated into physical form and their duty is to guide, guard, protect and watch over you as you complete your sacred mission here on Earth.

In general, angels are powerful Divine messengers and can assist us with every aspect of our lives. Angels have no bodies, egos, or agendas and make no judgments about us. They are always happy to assist us with our path and journey. This is why I feel very comfortable working with them and I can trust that whenever they come in during a reading, I know that the information is always for the highest good and purpose for that individual, including myself.

Some angels have a very obvious gender and some do not. People who are sensitive to energy may get a feeling that a particular angel is more feminine or more masculine. However, you may not always be able to tell the gender because that angel may be androgynous. Many people see flashes of pure white light and this is the energy of the angels that you can see with your physical eye. These flashes are referred to as "angel lights." If you have never experienced seeing angel lights, try this exercise:

> When you get ready for bed, put on your favorite pajamas, climb into bed and get really comfortable. Have an open mind and attitude when you shut off the light. Allow your eyes to adjust to the dark and either silently to yourself or out loud ask the angels to please show you their angel lights now, and remember to say thank you. Quickly scan your whole room for those flashes or sparks of light. Bright, solid white flashes are angelic energy and colored sparks of light may be archangels, guides or Ascended Masters. Be quick and pay attention for they only last for a few seconds. You are now seeing the energy of your angels with your physical eyes. Very cool if you ask me!

The Angelic Realm

Now let's talk about who resides in the angelic realm. There are different tiers within the angelic realm, but we will focus on guardian angels, archangels, Ascended Masters, spirit guides, fairies and deceased loved ones.

Guardian Angels

The Guardian Angels are the closest to all human beings and most people have at least two guardian angels. A person can have more than two depending on their life's purpose path and their love and passion for the angels.

Of the two guardian angels, one is usually very loud, outspoken, extroverted and a bit pushy. I refer to this angel as your "kick-butt" angel. I say "kick-butt" because this angel's job is to lovingly push you into action and can help you with day-to-day life. This angel can motivate you to work on projects, complete tasks and move you forward on your spiritual path. The other angel is usually very soft spoken, introverted and quiet. I call this angel your "nurturing and emotional angel" because this angel is very connected to your heart and emotions. When you are down in the dumps, needing more emotional support or are just stressed with life, this is the angel to call. They will put their loving arms and energy all around you to lift your spirit and comfort you. Combined together, these two beings of light are powerful and will guide you with your life and your life's purpose.

Your angels have names, personalities, intelligence and a wonderful sense of humor. I recall, while working at home on a new lecture, I started to draft the class lecture on my flip chart. I called on Archangel Michael for assistance (he's my boss) and please keep in mind that Michael is considered the patron saint of police officers. I said "Michael, are you here helping me, buddy, or are you goofing off somewhere? I need you to help me now please!" A couple of minutes went by and then my phone rang. On the other line, I heard,

"Hello, is this Elizabeth Foley?" I responded, "Yes, this is she." The voice on the other end of the phone continued, "This is the Nashua Police Department and we are conducting a fund raiser..." and proceeded to give me all the details of their event.

After completing the conversation, I had to laugh out loud and with hands on my hips and my foot tapping, I said in a very loud and firm voice, "Archangel Michael, thank you for validating that you're here with me and helping," and I had to pay $25.00 for that validation. Even today this story brings a smile to my face and makes me laugh.

The angels are powerful beings of love and light. They are easy to work with and all they ask in return is a simple thank you!

Your guardian angels' mission is to use their special knowledge of you to provide the basic support and guidance you need to lead a balanced, healthy and harmonious life. Angels have the ability to look past our surface personality, limitations and the human mistakes that we make and they hold unconditional love for us. Later in the book, I will share with you how you can get your own guardian angels' names. It's simple and easy!

Archangels

There are many different types of angels in addition to your guardian angels. Another category of angels is the archangels. There are many different archangels and in fact no one really knows how many there are. The angel dictionaries seem to be getting bigger with each new edition that comes out.

In general, archangels are the managers and supervisors of our guardian angels and are more powerful. Each archangel has their own specialty and it is helpful to learn which function each archangel handles so that you will know whom to call upon in time of need. Even if you can't remember that Archangel Michael is the protector, you only have to ask for the angel of protection. Michael knows his job and will step forward to assist you. The only thing you need to remember is to ask for help. For a list of archangels and their areas of expertise, please refer to the Guide to Archangels in the appendix section of this book.

Ascended Masters

The term Ascended Masters is a new age designation that means awakening to the divine within and being enlightened. The Masters are highly evolved beings who have achieved enlightenment. They are the great spiritual healers, leaders and teachers of the world. They have lived here on earth and have walked in our shoes, but now reside in the spirit world where they have ascended to a heavenly dimension, helping everyone who needs them. They are available for love, guidance, support and information whenever you call on them. They can act as a spiritual mentor or even as a personal guide.

Along with God and the angels, these Masters will never violate our free will. They await our decision to call on them and when we do, it is at that instant that they come to us. They have the ability to be with everyone who calls on them simultaneously, as Jesus promised, "I am with you always." The most famous Ascended Masters include Jesus the Christ,

Buddha, Moses, Krishna, Kuthumi, Mohammed, Mother Mary, St. Germaine, and Quan Yin just to name a few.

Spirit Guides

Guides are evolved spiritual beings whom you contracted with before you incarnated here on Earth. Guides can assist you with your spiritual path and evolution. Often your intention will attract specific spirit guides who can help you with your soul work and mission. Because they have lived as humans, they still possess an ego. However, from schooling that they received on the other side, they are aware of their ego and have learned to control and manage their ego state and personal agendas. Spirit guides have different frequencies and live in a different dimension. Spirit Guides can be people close to us from a past life(s) or deceased loved ones.

Fairies and Elemental Beings

Yes, fairies and elementals do exist. In general, they are great healers and can offer guidance and healing to those who call on them. Fairies are the nature angels and are different than angels. Unlike the angels, fairies have bodies, wings, and have a different vibration. Like a spirit guide, fairies also possess egos, so "please" and "thank you" are a must when working with them. They tend to be a little mistrusting of humans because of how we have treated the environment and its creatures. So speak kindly and with respect for them and you might be surprised when they show up and offer their assistance.

Deceased Loved Ones

Deceased loved ones are just that, deceased loved ones. Some may have died before you were born and have agreed to serve as your guardian spirit for the family. Deceased loved ones can act in the capacity of a guardian angel by surrounding you with love, whispering guidance in your ear and bringing many gifts to your life. Some deceased loved ones remain because they need to fulfill their life purpose by vicariously working through you. Sometimes this is their assignment in life for their namesake. Deceased parents may spend more time with the most troubled sibling, and they devote their time on earth to gently support and guide family members through life. Most deceased loved ones are grandparents, parents, siblings and beloved friends. Once this person has crossed over to the spirit world, they are given a choice to be a spirit guide. If they choose to be a guide, they then receive special training in the afterlife about how to be a spirit guide or guardian spirit. Like spirit guides, deceased loved ones still possess an ego upon passing and they receive training that emphasizes that they are not to interfere with your free will or make decisions for you. Your deceased loved ones are there to give you general advice, comfort, and at times warning and protection. However, for life purpose questions and clarification, ask God and the angels. Go all the way up for this.

When conducting an angel reading, you need to know who to call on for help and guidance. Here are a few basic rules of thumb to follow:

♥ For life purpose path clarity and direction, call on Archangel Michael.

♥ For assistance with day-to-day activities, ask for help from your guardian angels.

♥ When dealing with grief over a deceased loved one, call on that deceased being directly.

♥ If seeking a spiritual mentor, ask the spirit world (Masters and guides of all kinds) to begin to work with you.

2

CHAPTER

WHAT IS AN ANGEL READING

An angel reading is a great way to start a dialogue and exchange with your angelic team. An angel reading can consist of using divination tools like pendulums, dowsing rods, tarot and oracle cards to just name a few. Do you need these tools? The answer is "No!" because you are the tool. Conducting an angel reading also involves listening to the intuitive messages and information that your angels and guides provide for you.

When I use cards for a reading, I prefer using oracle cards. The word oracle means getting information from a Divine source and oracle cards unlike tarot cards, allow you to build your intuition more. In my opinion, oracle cards feel more positive, are easy to work with and these types of cards work well with other cards and tools that you may already have.

An angel reading is about connecting with the angelic realm and listening to the intuitive messages that are received along with the cards or your divination tools. Depending upon the needs of the person you are reading, the angels may even prescribe homework such as clearing their chakras or etheric cord cutting. For example, I was conducting a reading on a woman whose name was Sally (not her real name). The cards that came up in her angel session were the "Soulmate" and "Sexuality" cards. If I had simply followed the message from the book that came with the deck of cards, I would have said that her lover was sexually abusing her. However, I talked telepathically to my angelic team and asked for guidance regarding the meaning and how to deliver the message. What I received back surprised me. My team said, "Ask her what she does for work." Of course I argued with them and said, "Stop playing games with me and tell me the meaning behind these cards." They said again, "Ask her what she does for work." The arguing continued until I finally gave in. I looked at Sally and asked her what she did for work.

She replied back, "I am an attorney." I was still not getting the message, so I asked her to tell me a little more. She said, "I am an attorney for the District Attorney's Office and I work on child sex abuse cases."

Bingo, the download came directly in and showed me that all the human suffering that she was dealing with was now affecting her soulmate relationship. As she listened to what I was saying, the fairies came in and proceeded to prescribe homework to help her. Fairies are wonderful teachers and creative healers. They said that she had construction paper at home, and she should cut out a big purple heart. She should then cut out a smaller pink heart and write her first name on it, put both hearts together and pin them to her blouse for 24 hours.

Interesting, I thought. Hmm... how I am going to explain this one?

I believe in trusting and speaking from the heart. I inquired if she did indeed have construction paper at home. She did! She said that she keeps some craft supplies for her young nieces and nephews that come to visit.

Then I shared with her that the fairies wanted to help her heal her love life. She said in a very loud (almost screaming) voice, "What fairies?" "Yes," I said, "They do exist and are offering their services." At this point, I must have looked like I had six heads instead of one. I thought, "Well, let's finish what I have begun," and explained to her about creating the two hearts and pinning them to her blouse for 24 hours. She listened with this look of puzzlement on her face and then asked, "Why?"

I did not have an answer for her so I asked the fairies, "Why?" This is what they told me: "This exercise will help her bring back the element of play in her life and keep her heart open to love. Whenever she walks by a window or mirror and sees her reflection with the pink and purple heart, it will remind her to keep her focus on her heart and love."

I thought that was pretty cool and clever. I explained everything to her and, as always, left the decision of whether to follow this Divine guidance and homework to my client. This is a very important part of an angel reading, to honor and respect every person's free will and choice regarding their response to the information given.

PSYCHIC GIFTS

Are you ready for a test? Do you know the difference between someone who is psychic and someone who is intuitive? Now take a moment to think about this before you continue. When you think you know the answer, then you may continue to read.

Everyone is psychic or has psychic potential. There is no exception to this truth except when someone believes that they need to be a "special" person or possess "special powers." They will automatically block themselves from tapping into their own gifts. So everyone is psychic but not everyone is intuitive.

Someone who is psychic can perceive information and energy around someone and read the energy; they will simply convey what they receive. An intuitive is someone who assesses the core beingness of the person they are reading and does a check in with their spiritual team, asking, "Is this something I need to share or just to know?" The intuitive assesses the mental and emotional status of the person and then asks, "Can this person handle what I am getting?" The bottom line is that an intuitive knows when to speak and when to stay silent. Just because you get information does not mean you always have to share it!

So the more you know and understand energy, the more you will begin to understand your own psychic gifts. As you exercise your psychic gifts by playing with them all the time, you will strengthen them. One example of playing with and even strengthening your psychic gifts is to predict who is calling on the phone before you answer it or look at the caller ID. The next time you are waiting at a red light, try to guess how many seconds it will be before the red light changes to green. Take a deck of regular playing cards and pull one out and without looking at the card, get a sense and feel of the color, the number or image on the card. Once you think you have it, then turn the card over for validation. These are just some simple and fun ways to begin to awaken your own psychic potential.

Your Psychic Gifts

Your psychic gifts are connected with the chakras. Chakras are spinning wheels or vortexes of energy centered within your body's energy field. You need them to stay alive. They feed life-force energy to the body and nourish all the cells and organs of the body.

Your psychic gifts are also referred to as the "four clairs." The "four clairs" are clairvoyance, clairaudience, clairsentience and claircognizance. Many people receive messages and information through nonverbal means such as visions, feelings, or even knowingness; not everyone hears angelic voices as audible sounds. Your psychic gifts are God's gift to you! Now let us review the "four clairs."

Clairvoyance

Receiving visions, images and mental pictures is called clairvoyance and it means, "clear seeing." This clair is associated with the Third Eye chakra for spiritual sight and the color of this chakra is indigo blue.

Some clairvoyant experiences include corner-of-eye visions, meditation visions and invocations, dream visitations or apparition experiences. The visions may come to you as single snapshot pictures inside or outside of your mind, or you can see miniature scenes similar to a mental movie. These images may be black-and-white or in full color and they can be literal or symbolic. If you tend to be strongly clairvoyant and are receiving a lot of images and symbols, you may want to start keeping a journal. Study your symbols and ask your angelic team to reveal to you if they are literal or symbolic. It is important to pay attention because if they are symbolic, you need to ask for the interpretation and keep track of this information. Why? Some of the images or symbols and their meanings will be pertinent only for you and no one else. For example, when I see a pond with stagnant water over someone's head or around them, for me it means that there is something that is stagnant in their life. Now you may ask how I came to that understanding of the meaning. It's simple.

I was doing a reading on a woman some time ago and she

was questioning her marriage. She spoke of her emotional challenges with her husband and wondered what the angels had to say to her.

As she conveyed her unhappiness, I saw a pond above her head and thought about what this could mean. This image did not make sense to me. If I took the meaning literally I could say, "Go swimming," and that would fix everything. However, that did not feel right nor make a whole lot of sense. I explained to the angels that I was not going to tell this woman to go swimming while she was in the midst of an emotional breakdown and possible divorce. I asked the angels to give me more information because what they were showing me did not seem appropriate.

Then I heard inside of my head, "Go closer to the pond" and in my mind's eye I watched myself walk around the pond. I could see matted down grass, broken tree branches and old dried up leaves. As I moved in closer to the pond and looked into the water, it appeared to be very still. There was no life to the water. There was no movement in the water and no fish. There was nothing growing in the water, not even one lily pad. The water was very stagnant and I shared with the angels what I was seeing and experiencing. They said, "Like the pond, her marriage is stagnant. There is no life left to the marriage and no passion or compassion."

I am not sure why I had to work so hard to understand this message, but sometimes it happens. Now when I see this stagnant pond, I know that something is stagnant in that person's life.

Another important aspect of being clairvoyant is receiving

messages through dreams. These visions and information can also come during our dreamtime. If you are a vivid dreamer, pay attention to the messages and symbolism and keep the interpretations in a journal.

Clairaudience

The next "clair" focuses on sounds, voices and words. This type of communication is called clairaudience, which means "clear hearing" and is associated with the Ear chakra for spiritual hearing. The color of this chakra is magenta. Some forms of clairaudience include hearing your named called, music, ringing in one of your ears, hearing an inner voice, a warning or possibly hearing an angel or deceased loved one's voice. The sounds, voices or words can either be heard with your physical ears or often times you will hear the voices emanating from within the side of your head. The sounds or voices can resemble your own voice or they may be in a very different voice. Angelic voices are consistently loving and supportive. Hearing your name called when no one is there means that you are a natural born medium. A medium is someone who has the ability to connect with the spirit world and bring in messages from deceased loved ones. Everyone is psychic, but not everyone is a medium.

Clairsentience

The third way to receive messages and information is through our emotions, physical sensations and gut feelings. This is called clairsentience and it means, "clear feeling." This "clair" is associated with the solar plexus or the third chakra, and the color of this energy center is bright yellow.

A clairsentient person receives information through their gut feelings and hunches, such as a tightening of the jaw, fists or stomach. Some common clairsentient occurrences involve sensing a presence with you, feeling someone sitting on your bed or around you, feeling your ear being pinched or a wing brushing against your skin (face, arms or hands), sensing air pressure and temperature changes, experiencing sudden pain or illness, the tightening of your stomach or jaw, a gut feeling that something is not quite right, smelling things like the scent of a flower, perfume, food, smoke (cigarettes or tobacco) or some other disembodied scent. Many times these smells mean that someone who has passed is now visiting from the spirit world and this is their calling card. The spirit world knows I like food, so there have been times when they will give me a smell or taste of a certain food like chocolate chip cookies when there are no cookies around. These smells and tastes are a sign from a deceased loved one to let you know that they are around you.

This is a wonderful "clair" to have. However, if you tend to be very clairsentient and sensitive to energy, you will need to practice some spiritual hygiene like clearing your aura, chakras and dissolving energy cords on a daily basis.

Claircognizance

We can also receive messages and guidance as a "knowingness," whereby we are given thoughts, ideas and inner certainty directly from God's universal intelligence. This type of psychic gift is called claircognizance, which means "clear knowing." This "clair" is associated with the Crown or seventh chakra which deals with spirituality. The color of this energy center is violet, purple or white.

In general, men are frequently claircognizant and many of them do not realize that they naturally receive detailed and accurate information from God and angels. You can ask a claircognizant a question on almost any topic and within seconds they will give you information on that topic. If you ask them, "How did you know this?" they will usually respond, "I don't know!" Claircognizants know information without knowing how they know and the information is largely discounted and doubted. This is a powerful "clair" to have, but it is the most difficult and challenging one, because it takes enormous TRUST to state what you are receiving for information and messages.

MEETING YOUR ANGELS

Everyone has angels, there really is no exception to this rule. Before learning how to conduct an angel reading, it is best for you to meet your angels. Meeting your angels and getting their names is simple and easy!

First, find a place where you will not be disturbed. If necessary, let your family members know that you need to have some quiet space for a little while.

Next, place yourself in a comfortable position and close your eyes. Focus your attention on your breath. Breathing helps to calm and center you. While you are relaxing your whole body, ask your guardian angels to come in close to you. Pay attention to how many angelic presences you sense or just ask, "How many guardian angels are with me?" Get a sense or feel for how many and if they are male or female.

Please do not second guess yourself, just trust the first thing that comes to you.

Remember, angels have names and some names are angelic, some are plain like our names and some are unusual. If you would like to receive your angel's name, here is a simple exercise you can try at home:

> Focus your intention on getting the names of your angels. Become aware of the angels that surround you and ask, "Angels, please tell me the name of the guardian angel on my left shoulder," then wait for a response. Trust whatever you get. Do the same again for the angel on your right shoulder and trust. There, it's just that simple!

In case you have some doubts, you can always ask the angels to validate their names. Just say, "Angels, I think one of your names is Jessica and if this is true and accurate, please give me a clear concrete sign today and thank you." Then pay attention to everything. It could come in a message from an email or even a stranger. If you want a very specific sign, you can instruct them on what you would like. For example, I like to work with numbers. So, if I need validation I will tell them that if the answer is "Yes" and accurate, then show me "three consecutive fours in a row... 444," and if it is "No" or inaccurate, then show me "three consecutive nines in a row... 999."

Let your imagination guide you as you come up with ways in which the angels can assure you that you have discovered their names.

PREPARING YOURSELF

Even when doing a reading for yourself, you will need to prepare. Preparing yourself for a reading means that you are clearing yourself energetically and creating sacred space within you as well as all around you. Beings in the angelic realm and spirit world vibrate at a much higher level than you do and that is why not everyone sees angels, fairies, Masters or deceased loved ones. Therefore, it is important, if not vital, to begin to take good care of yourself energetically, practicing good spiritual hygiene. This will help you to match your vibration to the angelic realm so that you have a stronger and firmer connection and can receive messages more easily.

Here are some ways that you can prepare yourself:

Chakra Clearing and Balancing

There are many different ways to clear, balance and align your chakras. These are just a few suggestions.

♥ Listen to chakra clearing audio tapes or CDs.

- ♥ Ask Archangel Raphael to enter your body and cleanse, balance and align all chakras.

- ♥ Deep chakra clearing with the angels (the chakra clearing technique can be found in the appendix of my first book, *Awakening the Lightworker Within*).

- ♥ Command your chakras to open, align and balance now. This method uses your high mind energy to direct your chakras (energy centers) like we used to back in the time of Atlantis.

- ♥ Sound/vibration therapy.

- ♥ Reiki and other energy work.

Increasing Your Energy and Vibration

It is important to keep your energy high and positive. Bring in Divine energy to keep your own energy positive. If you are not sure how to do this, try these helpful tips.

- ♥ Breathing naturally raises your vibration, calms down the body and slows down the mind or mental chatter.

- ♥ Yoga, Tai Chi, Qigong.

- ♥ Prayer, meditation and toning.

Grounding

Being grounded helps you to stay focused on the present moment and allows you to feel more connected with your body. If you have a hard time grounding yourself, below are some ways to help you easily ground and enjoy your reading experience even more.

♥   Simply breathing is grounding.

♥   Chocolate or water (yes, chocolate, "food of the gods").

♥   Visualize tree roots extending from your feet going into Mother Earth.

♥   Perform the Cross Arms Technique: While sitting, cross your arms and place your hands on your kneecaps for ten seconds. Then swap your hands (your arms are still crisscrossed) and hold your kneecaps for another ten seconds. Next, move your crossed arms and hands to your shoulders and hold for ten seconds, then change hands for another ten seconds. This helps to ground in the energy from your meridians, which are smaller, more complex energy centers.

Energy Cord Cutting

Every person with whom you have had an emotional experience, positive or negative, stays connected to you through a psychic etheric cord. These cords are created from your emotions such as fear (fear of losing something) or wanting something. You have probably heard of the term psychic vampires. A psychic vampire is a person who drains you of energy. If you have ever experienced this, then you were "corded." If you have enough cords, you can experience physical symptoms. Shoulder pain or stomach upset are a few examples. Clairvoyants can see the cords with their physical eyes. Clairsentients can feel the cords and cords can even show up on an aura photograph, appearing like black strings or cords. To remove cords, here are some simple techniques to try:

- ♥ Ask Archangel Michael to use his blue flaming sword of love to cut away all cords of attachment to you. You may also ask him to sever only those cords that drain you of your energy.

- ♥ Use etheric scissors or an etheric machete to cut the cords yourself.

- ♥ Call forth the violet flame of transmutation and direct the violet flame to dissolve away all cords or specify what cords you wish to remove.

Removing Negativity and Entities

When negativity hits your aura (your energy field), the negative energy tends to stick like mud or a post-it-note to your auric field. If you have enough mud or post-it-notes stuck to your energy field, this can cause depression and possibly physical illness. Entities are thought forms of fear and fear thoughts can create entities. Entities can be tricky and they have either very little or no light. An entity does not look like an angel or a person. They look more like a blob, spider, crab, snake, dark cloud, or even a parasite or gargoyle. Entities are attracted to people who are fearful or negative and tend to attach to people who think about evil or who have addictions to alcohol, cigarettes and drugs. Entities can move from person to person. Even the dark likes the light. To remove negativity, including entities, here are some suggestions:

- ♥ Invoke Archangel Michael saying, "Archangel Michael, please be with me now and connect to my energy and essence. Michael, please clear me both inside and out, all of my chakras and para-chakras, physical body and subtle bodies, conscious-subconscious and super-conscious mind, my higher self, soul and oversoul, my home and everything in my home, my vehicle and everything in my vehicle, of all excessive energy, negativity, earthbound spirits, entities, lower vibrational energies and entities, psychic dirt, debris, slime, parasites and any being, energy or entity that is not from the Light or has been reprogrammed by the Light or not 100% pure Light, all negative elementals, devices and implants, please take all of this back to the source of Light now and thank you."

♥   Clear the chakras with the angels or the violet flame.

Shielding

There are literally hundreds of ways to shield your energy and until humans can hold more light and keep our vibration high, we need to shield. When someone comes to you for a reading, you never know what or whom they are coming in with, so shield please! Here are some powerful techniques that you can use:

♥   White Light – Visualize a tall tube of white light surrounding you that goes from Earth all the way up to the heavens, and there is an opening at the top to allow the pure white light and energy to flow in and all around you. This light is pure Divine energy and the light insulates you from negative energy or entity attachments. This light and energy allows you to be loving and compassionate with others while shielding you from negative energy.

- ♥ White Bubble with Oily Consistency on the Outside – This allows negativity and etheric cords to slide off instead of becoming attached to you.

- ♥ Visualize Archangel Michael's shield all around you and ask him to enfold you in his mighty wings.

- ♥ Place tall panes of mirrors all around you that go from the ground up to the heavens and set the intention that only love, positive thoughts and energy are allowed to pass through, everything else is reflected back out and neutralized by the universe.

Now that you are ready, it is time to prepare your own oracle cards.

6

CHAPTER

PREPARING YOUR CARDS

It is important to know your cards. When you are conducting an angel reading, the angels may bring your attention to one small detail on the card. Their message may have nothing to do with the written message on the card. It could be a very simple image, the color, one single word or the complete message on the card.

Since you never know where your particular deck has come from (whether it is new, direct from the factory, through friends or even a yard sale), it is necessary to clear and bless your deck. For each deck of cards that you own, no matter what type of deck you have (tarot, animal, angel, fairy or any other deck), you need to clear your cards, infuse your cards with your heart energy and bless them with your intention and prayer.

Clearing Your Cards

Even if your card deck is brand new you will need to clear your cards. Periodically (every ten or so readings), you will need to do the same clearing process. If anyone picks up your cards and touches or plays with them, you will again need to clear your cards. Why, you might ask? Remember, everything is energy and your cards can pick up excess, negative or funky energy.

There are many different ways to clear your oracle cards and here are several methods to do this:

♥ Spread your card deck out and allow either the sun or moonbeam energy to bathe your cards for at least 24 hours.

♥ If you practice Reiki, you can use the Reiki symbols to clear your deck.

♥ Use your breath and intention.

♥ Burn sage and fan the smoke from the sage over the spread out deck.

♥ Place a clear quartz crystal on top of your deck and set the intention of having the crystal absorb all heavy energy and negativity.

♥ Ask Archangel Michael to clear the cards for you and then say thank you.

Blessing Your Cards

Blessing your cards with your heart energy and intention is

just as important as clearing your cards. You only need to do this once.

With your cleared deck in your hands, fan them out and place them on top of your heart. Next, set your intention for the kind of readings you want to conduct with your cards. Then create an intentional, purposeful prayer that infuses and blesses your cards. Here is an example of an easy prayer that you can use. Feel free to modify it to suit your particular beliefs and comfort level.

Example prayer:

> *"Dear God and Angels, I, (state your name), bless and infuse these cards with the energy of my heart. The pure energy of light, love and truth. I ask that the information and the messages received during readings of these cards are always true, accurate and provide healing to all those who seek out truth, wisdom, guidance and healing. Amen"*

This is only an example, but you understand what I am getting at. Ask your angelic spiritual team what type of prayer and blessing would be appropriate for you to use and then just TRUST!

Knowing Your Cards

The next step is to know your cards and understand the vast meanings of each one. I highly suggest that you create a special reading notebook. Sit quietly with your cards and ask your angels to work with you.

With your team assembled and your notebook by your side, hold and look at each card individually. Begin to notice all the details of each card and look at the word or message on the card. Next, get a sense and feel for each card. Does it make you happy or sad? Does it feel like a serious or lighthearted type of card? Pay attention to details!

If there is a book or booklet that comes with your deck of cards, read it at least once and then ask your angels to give you more information, messages and guidance about each card. Keep a journal of any other impressions and information that you receive.

Your angels will supply you with other meanings to the cards. For example, in one deck of angel cards that I use there is a card with a beautiful golden angel blowing her trumpet and the theme of the card is Music. The booklet that came with the cards talked about listening to music, creating music or even making a musical instrument. However, when I connected with the angels, they gave me another new meaning, the card represents Archangel Gabriel who is often depicted as blowing her trumpet.

Do not rely on the book or booklet that came with your deck. If you do, the message that needs to be conveyed may be very incomplete or even inaccurate. Be open to your own understanding or interpretation of the cards, for the angels will often surprise you!

When I first started doing readings, I did rely on the booklet. Then one day the angels decided to show me what a powerful connection I truly had. I always doubted myself and the angels knew that this needed to change.

While conducting a reading on a colleague at work, the

person asked one final question, "Elizabeth, will this company allow me to do my heart's passion?" I had no idea what her heart's passion was and I felt shy about asking her. Even though her reading had been going very smoothly, I now hit a roadblock. When I laid out the cards for this question, they did not make any sense. My client looked at the cards, trying to help me with the interpretation. How embarrassing, now the client needs to help me. I could not make any sense of the meaning and neither could she. However, what happened next was pretty amazing and it opened my eyes wide and helped me to trust my connection and inner guidance.

After a few minutes of struggling, the angels began speaking to me. They told me that this person was going to be leaving the company soon. I was quite surprised by this because the person was fairly new to the company.

I had to trust now and told the person what the angels had just said.

She said, almost screaming, "What! I just got here and I am very happy. I have no intentions of leaving and I like it here very much." Then she inquired when she would be leaving the company.

Feeling very intimidated, nervous and stupid, I asked when this change would be happening. The angels showed me in my mind's eye a movie. They showed me a white building with red colored letters for the name of the company but I could not clearly see the individual letters. I saw my client walking very confidently, professionally dressed in black, wearing gold jewelry and carrying a dark-colored briefcase.

While watching the movie play out, she walked down a hallway that was located on the second floor and windows were off to her right side. When I looked out the windows, I could see trees with green leaves and it appeared to be a beautiful summer day. Then the angels showed me the number "8," which could mean 8 days, 8 weeks, 8 months, the 8th month (her reading was done mid-July... the 7th month) or it could mean 8 years. However, it did not seem that the change would take that long. I shared with her what I was seeing and explained as clearly as possible about the number eight.

She replied, "I am not looking for another job. If the change was going to be eight days, eight weeks or even in the eighth month, which is just around the corner, I would need to be looking now, Elizabeth. And I am not looking for anything."

Listening to her words, I heard the angels say in a very soft and loving voice, "She will make a lot of money." I also shared this information, but by this time my client seemed very doubtful of me and her reading. I felt lower than low. I truly believed that I blew it. However, that impression was about to change.

July came and went, and mid-August arrived, the 8th month. This same client pulled me into her office and said, "Sit down, I need to talk to you about the reading that you gave me a few weeks ago."

I felt apprehensive, but willing to listen. She told me that she had been working from home at the end of July and Staples® contacted her for a new position. The position would fulfill her heart's passion and after going back and forth with personnel trying to arrange an interview, the manager said, "What kind of money would it take for you to make this move?" The client said to me, "Elizabeth, I made up some ridiculous amount of money and they agreed to it!" Not only was her career transition happening in the eighth month, but the location was also eight minutes away from her home.

I think this experience was pretty cool and it helped me with trusting more. I still use the cards during a reading, but I let the angels talk to me first and then the cards usually validate everything we have already covered.

Remember, the angels want success for you and take great enjoyment and pleasure from connecting with you. You are a Divine messenger and your angels want to work with you. You only need to invite them in. Trust and let the magic begin!

7

CHAPTER

ANGEL READING PROCESS

A n angel reading involves the use of oracle cards, which are very ancient divination tools. Divination tools include oracle cards, pendulums and dowsing rods. Angel oracle cards are positive and can be used every day. An angel reading is a quick, fun and easy way to connect and start a dialogue with your angels.

The angel reading process may at first seem complicated, but once you get the hang of it, it's truly quite simple. It's just like getting on a bike. Think about all the steps you need to take to get on your bike and ride it. The same concept works for readings as well.

In this chapter we will discuss the angel reading process. In the following chapters we will review some card spreads and explore some possible interpretations and meanings.

To conduct an angel reading, there is a 15-step process. Again, once you begin to practice these steps, it will become easy and flow.

The Angel Reading Process

♥   Clear and shield yourself.

♥   Clear your cards.

♥   Breathe and center yourself.

♥   Ask Archangel Michael and the Holy Spirit to be with you and preside over this reading for (say the person's full name) highest good. Remember to say "thank you."

♥   Connect with your angels first, then the other person's angels.

♥   Bless the reading with a prayer (this can be optional).

♥   Formulate the question. Short and simple questions work the best. For example, "Angels, is it time for me to look for a new job?" or "Angels, is this the right time for me to make a residential move?" or "Angels, what do you want me to know about my marriage?"

♥   Shuffle the cards while asking your question at least three times silently. Three times so that you are clear and the angels are clear about what you are inquiring about. Never change your question mid-way. If you need to change your question say, "Angels, cancel and clear that question and now this is my new question."

♥   Ask how many cards to pull. Trust what you get unless you get a number like 25, then you might want to ask again. When in doubt, 3-5 cards are always perfect!

♥ Pull the cards out of the deck with whatever method you choose to select the cards. Here are a few options for pulling the cards. You can pick from the top, middle, bottom, cut the deck, spread the cards out and either you or your client can choose the cards or my favorite, pick the cards that stick out of the deck when you shuffle.

♥ Lay the cards out and be mindful of how you do this. If you tend to pull the cards and they are always upside down to you, the reader, the upside down cards mean that there is a blockage of some kind and every reading you do would be inappropriate or inaccurate. Always lay the cards down from left to right unless you are guided differently.

♥ Begin to see the Big Picture and read the cards from left to right. If you are working with multiple decks, read the same way, first from left to right and then from top to bottom.

♥ Ask your angels for additional information. TRUST and do not JUDGE. You are that Divine Messenger and you are to deliver the angels' messages with as much love and compassion as you can. It is not your place to judge anyone.

♥ If necessary, give homework and healing, just be open!

♥ When finished, clear the cards and ask Archangel Michael to cut all the cords from you to the people you have read, then thank him.

Doing an angel reading can be very powerful and even provide healing for some people. Because you are the Divine Messenger, trust what you get and do not make judgements. I have heard just about everything and you probably will too. Sometimes people come in with infidelity concerns, addictions, sexuality issues and other private matters.

You are there to make a connection. Deliver the message with love and compassion, without judgment.

8
CHAPTER

DIFFERENT CARD SPREADS

There are many different card spreads that you can experiment with. It's an individualistic and intuitive process. Many of the books or booklets that are included in your card sets offer instructions and different card spreads.

If you enjoy learning and playing with different spreads, there is a fabulous book called *Illustrated Tarot Spreads* that you may enjoy reading.

The following spreads are widely used and include Daily Message, Personal Reflection, Future Outlook, Divine Guidance, Sacred Body and the Chakra spread. Let's talk about each one of these spreads and remember to trust what feels right to you.

Daily Message (1-2 cards)

This reading involves asking the angels what you need to know about the upcoming day. It's simple and easy.

Personal Reflection (1-3 cards)

Using the same procedure as above, you will ask for guidance at the end of the day. Your intention is to ask what you need to understand about your day and reflect upon what you receive.

Future Outlook (12 cards)

This spread involves asking your angels to give you an outline of what will happen over the next 12 months. You will pull a card for each month to get an overall view of what is in store for you.

Divine Guidance (4 cards)

This spread centers on asking guidance on a particular situation or problem and requires four cards. The first card represents your situation, the second card highlights the obstacle or challenge, the third card provides you with Divine guidance in order to move through the challenge and the fourth card represents the likely outcome if you follow the angels' guidance.

Sacred Body (4 cards)

This spread requires four cards. The first card gives you information about your spiritual body, the second card represents the mental body, the third card relates to your emotional body and the last card corresponds to your physical body.

Chakra Spread (7 cards)

If you understand the chakras then you will thoroughly enjoy this spread. The first card gives information about your root chakra (survival and getting basic needs met), the second card provides information about your sacral chakra (physical desires), the third card represents your solar plexus chakra (power and control challenges), the fourth card gives information about your heart chakra (relationships, love, and people attachments), the fifth card relates to your throat chakra (speaking your truth and creativity), the sixth card provides information about your third eye chakra (doorway to clairvoyance) and the seventh card represents your crown chakra (spiritual growth and your Divine connection).

As you begin your readings, becoming more familiar and comfortable with the process, your angels will work with you, giving you other kinds of spreads. Again, TRUST and go with the flow.

INTERPRETING THE CARDS

There are many different ways to interpret the meanings of the cards. Here are some basic rules of thumb that you can follow:

♥ Look at each card.

♥ Notice all the details of the cards, especially the artwork and colors. The message could be contained within the art or card design instead of the text message on the card. Remember to be open and think outside the box.

♥ Read each card's message.

♥ Understand the position of each card.

♥ Notice a particular theme or story.

♥   Pay attention to any card that jumps or flies out of the deck. This is considered an extra card and has an important message that may be related to the question being asked or it may have an entirely different meaning.

♥   If a card is positioned upside down, it indicates that the person has a block.

♥   Ask your angels for guidance.

It is always important to be open to the angels' guidance on the meaning and interpretation of the cards.

If at any point during the reading you encounter a card or a combination of cards that do not make sense, just ask the angels for clarification. You can either listen for their response or you may draw an extra card(s), holding the intention of getting clarification. If the extra cards still do not make sense, you may need to clear your cards again.

In the next chapter, I share some of my readings to give you an idea of how this process works. Some readings were wild and hard for me to believe. But the more you trust and let go, the more the process will provide messages that are healing and very powerful. So trust and go with the flow. Have fun!

10

CHAPTER

ANGEL READING EXAMPLES

Nothing surprises me in a reading. The more you open to whatever unfolds, the more information will come through. In some instances the readings have been almost unbelievable. Included here are some true readings that I have personally conducted so that you may get a sense or feel of how all of this works.

Angel Reading Examples

X Marks the Spot

Not everyone you meet on Earth is from Earth. There are Earth Angels that walk amongst us. These are individuals who agreed to be here on planet Earth to help make a difference. Some Earth Angels are from the angelic realm, some from the fairy or elemental kingdom, others are wise ones which are the mystics, witches and shamans and some are star people. People who are clairvoyant are able to see energy and even wings on people. Yes, wings do exist and you really can see and feel them!

Now back to the reading. Cathy came for her reading without any particular questions in mind. So I brought my whole team in and when I sense that the person is an Earth Angel, I will tell them and explain what that means. Cathy is an Earth Angel, but a dabbler, meaning that she was a cross between two different types of Earth Angels. Cathy is a combination of three different types of energy.

I began by asking Cathy, as I do with many people, "When you were little and possibly even now, did you feel different or have a hard time fitting in?" She responded, "Most definitely." At first I saw angel wings on her and thought she was an incarnated angel, meaning that she was from the angelic realm. But then I saw a large body of water above her head. Seeing the combination of angel wings and water tells me that this person is an incarnated elemental, meaning from the fairy realm. More specifically, the water used to be her home. She is from the water, and she is what you call a mer-angel, a mermaid with angel wings and Cathy always needs to be near water.

I could also see stars above her head, which indicates that she is a star person. I asked Cathy if she liked looking at the stars and planets and she said, "Yes, I have always talked to the stars."

As we continued with her reading, it was very evident that Cathy did not see herself as being powerful or having psychic gifts. Since her angel reading was in my home, I was getting nudged by the angels to demonstrate to her just how gifted she actually was. I brought Cathy into my bathroom, which has a huge mirror. With no lights on and the door three quarters closed, only a little natural light coming in, I asked her to take a deep breath in and relax. I asked her to soften her vision and to scan about two inches all around her head with her physical eyes.

Cathy responded quickly, saying that she could see her wings and her aura. While we talked, I kept seeing with my peripheral vision a black box in the upper right hand corner of the bathroom. I got a little freaked out and asked Archangel Michael to clear the place but the box stayed there.

I told Cathy what I was seeing and she said that she saw it too. She asked if the box had an "X" on it. I said, "I do not see an "X" but the black is very present and strong." Cathy said that many times she has seen this "X" following her up in the sky and it felt very special to her.

At this point, the box came in very close to me and hovered right above my head. This made me feel very uncomfortable and I said, "Ok, that's enough, let's get out of here."

Not knowing what was happening, I asked Cathy if it would be all right if I phoned one of my colleagues to get some further information and validation about what had just happened and what it meant. Cathy was open to this and said it would be fine with her.

I quickly phoned one of my angel colleagues, Allison, and explained what just took place. She said that she could see the box and the "X" truly marks the spot. The box with the "X" was a homing device that was keeping track of Cathy.

Allison said that Cathy was not from Earth but from another star planet that looked similar to Earth but it was mostly comprised of water.

Cathy was delighted and could relate to everything being said.

I thanked Allison for her assistance. Cathy's face was glowing and she felt so much at peace. As Cathy's reading came to an end, I knew I would see her again.

A couple of months passed and Cathy phoned to say that she wanted to take my psychic development class. With an odd number of attendees for the class, I decided to participate so that everyone had a partner. It was the third eye opening that was very magical for me. I had everyone partner up and instructed them on how to open each other's third eye. Cathy did not have a partner so I volunteered to work with her.

I had no idea of the blessing that I was going to receive.

While Cathy worked on my third eye, I could clearly see her home planet. I just took in the whole experience. The planet looked like Earth with trees and small mountains. Then my attention went to a very large body of water and these beautiful etheric beings rose from the water. Telepathically they communicated with me and I knew that this was Cathy's star family. Their bodies were fluid like the water, but had a form and great love poured from them. I shared this with Cathy after the exercise and we were both overcome by joy and gratitude.

Hercules

Patti's (not her real name) reading was quite different and amazing all at the same time. During her angel reading, she wanted to receive clarification of her life purpose and direction. As Archangels Michael, Gabriel and Raziel came forth, I delivered their messages with love. Then I heard a firm male voice inside my head say, "She needs to work with Hercules again." I thought, "Good grief, what is this about Hercules?" At the time I did not know that Hercules was real. I only knew him as a fictional comic strip character, so this message seemed pretty far out there. Telepathically I said, "No, I am not going to tell her that." The message came again, and yes, sometimes I argue with the team. Hercules did not make any sense to me and I would feel like a fool just saying his name. Their message came again even stronger. "All right," I told my team, "I will tell her, but I feel foolish telling her to work with a comic strip character." Boy, was I surprised with what happened next.

Looking at my client, I conveyed the angels' message, "You need to work with Hercules again." The client almost fell off her seat. She apparently was hit very hard with this simple message which still did not make sense to me. I inquired if this message made sense to her and she said, "Yes." She continued, "I can't believe I am hearing this message," and proceeded to tell me that one year ago she was participating in a meditation session with other people. During her meditation Hercules came to her and said, "It is time for us to work together." In the days that followed, she talked with Hercules, but she became distracted and pulled away from connecting and talking with him.

Whenever I have a moment of doubt, I recall this reading and it reassures me that I just need to trust and let go. After the reading, I decided to do a little research on Hercules. I discovered that he is one of the seven Mighty Elohims.

Elohims are the Divine architects of the universe. This reading was a reconnection for her and a strong message for me to just trust.

Life's Work Path

I had a young gal call for a reading because she was in a state of perplexity due to a variety of different interests. One path led her to being a healer and working with energy medicine techniques, the other path led her to continue making sacred jewelry. As I brought the angels in, they guided me to my archangel deck. When I asked the question, I was guided to pull one card only. That one card was Archangel Raziel who was all draped in gold jewelry, holding a gold-studded jeweled staff. The theme of the card was "Clairvoyance," which had nothing to do with the question. Once the message was shared, the client laughed and said, "Elizabeth I have been asking this question for a few weeks and I kept getting this same card and it did not make sense to me." Now she understood her own message and was quite happy with the answer.

Remember, the angels' response can come in very simple ways. Her much needed answer came through the artwork, not the message on the card. The bottom line is to be open and observant; pay attention to everything.

Time to Go

I had a client call me first thing on a Monday morning, telling me that her husband was rushed to the hospital for an abdominal obstruction and to please pray for him. I said that I would put him on the prayer list and send healing angels and energy to him. On Wednesday morning she called me again and said that he just had emergency surgery and to please send extra angels to him. I agreed to keep him in my prayers and send healing energy his way. She phoned me the next day, saying her husband had to receive many transfusions. Early Friday morning she called me crying and upset. Her husband was bleeding internally somewhere and had not responded to the transfusions. As she continued crying, she said that the doctor wanted to perform exploratory surgery to find out the source of the bleeding, but she did not want to put her husband through anymore traumas. She asked, "What do the angels have to say?" I heard a soft and loving voice inside my head say, "Let him go." It was not my place to say this to her at this time. I said that I would meet her at the hospital right away. As I prepared to leave, I was guided to bring two different decks of cards with me.

Upon my arrival, the client met me and we spoke for sometime in the ICU waiting room. We talked at length about how quickly this scenario was playing out. She noticed that I had brought my oracle decks with me and asked again, "What do the angels have to say?" I asked my clients husband's angels and his higher self to join us for the reading. I was guided through my gut feeling to use both decks and to draw one card only from each deck. I had no idea what was going to happen next or how the angels were going to deliver the message.

As I prepared myself and the cards, I asked for extra guidance and told the angels that they needed to come in with a very clear message. Here is what they said through the cards.

I asked the question, "What does my client need to know now?" I drew one card from an angel deck, which was the

"Soulmate" card. The second card was from a fairy deck and the message on the card was "Letting Go." The messages on the cards told the whole story and I did not have to say one word. The client knew what it meant and understood what she needed to do. She spoke with her husband about the exploratory surgery, and he told her that he was tired of all of this and again said "no" to the surgery. My client somehow knew that she needed to gather the family together to say good-bye and after everyone visited and spoke their last words, the physician came in and tried to forcefully talk the patient into having the surgery. The patient became so upset that he had a massive stroke and died instantly.

Remember that you are a Divine messenger and not all readings are going to be light or fun. Trust that if you need to give such a reading, that you can do it with your whole team guiding you every step of the way.

A Little Boy Named Andrew

A young gal about 31 years old came for a reading and said that she had one question and only one question. As she sat down across from me she wanted to know if her little boy, Andrew, who was three years old, was going to stay here with her. She said that Andrew has had many health problems since birth and has had multiple surgeries.

Right away I heard, "No." I did not have the heart to just tell Mom "No." Telepathically I began talking with the angels, asking them to guide and work with me. I instructed them to guide me to the most appropriate deck of cards and to give me the right words to use. I made my intention to them very clear.

As I looked at six different decks of cards, the angels guided me to only one deck, which was the fairy deck. While shuffling the cards I formulated my question and asked, "What do we need to know about Andrew?"

I was guided to pull three cards and no more. The cards that came up were absolutely amazing and told the whole story. The three cards were "Vacation," "New Opportunity" and "Breaking Free."

I began to give a complete reading and felt that there was a vacation coming up by the end of the month. This vacation felt like it would have an amusement park theme and I was getting that this needed to be a family affair. Mom agreed saying, "Yes, the whole family is going to Disney World in Florida at the end of the month." "Great," I said, "Yes, please follow through to make this happen, it needs to be a family vacation."

As I focused on the second card of "New Opportunity," I felt that Andrew was going to be given another opportunity to go home. Remember that I told the angels to guide my every word for this reading.

While I pointed to the "New Opportunity" card, I spoke in a very soft and gentle voice saying, "Roughly within one month from returning from your vacation Andrew is going to be given another opportunity to go back home and right now the way he is feeling, he is choosing to go home." The "going home" came from the last card, "Breaking Free." Mom began to cry and reached for her handbag. She pulled out a photo of Andrew who looked like a little angel. She explained that Andrew was scheduled for yet another surgery shortly after coming back from vacation. She said, "Elizabeth, you don't know Andrew, but he constantly walks around the house and pulls on my clothes and says, "Mommy, it hurts too much to be here, I want to go home." We both began to cry but knew the message had to be delivered so that the family could enjoy whatever time Andrew had left. I also told Mom that this was how Andrew was feeling right now and that tomorrow he could wake up and say, "It's not that bad being here" and change his mind. There is always free will.

This reading shook my own core. My own angel training did not prepare me for this type of serious reading. I felt so unprepared. This was a strong confirmation and validation to me that my angelic team stands right beside me and guides me in all ways, including the right use of words.

It is my hope that you will never have to do a reading like this, but if you do, please trust your guidance, know that the angels are using you to deliver that message and that you might be the only one who can.

My Bikini Underwear

I always say that the spirit world knows everything. They can even tell you what color your underwear is. The spirit world decided to test my belief. I was asked to do a reading for a young gal, referred me by her mom, who was struggling with depression and an eating disorder. Sometimes during a reading mediumship may happen. Mediumship is the act of connecting with a decreased loved one and bringing in messages from the spirit world.

More than halfway through the reading, the young girl's deceased grandfather on Mom's side of the family decided to join us. He expressed deep concern for his granddaughter, but she did not believe that he was here. Knowing that she did not believe that he was here, he showed me a pair of bikini underwear hanging on a plastic hanger.

"Great," I am thinking, "I am dealing with a peeping tom type of spirit." However, that was not the case. I asked the young gal if she wore bikini underwear. She said, "What, why are you asking me this?" Her mom, seated on the couch listening, quickly turned to face us and said, "Elizabeth, where is this going?" I first needed validation from her daughter before I could explain. So I asked her daughter again, "Do you wear bikini underwear?"

Her face turned ten shades of red as she said, "Yes, I do." Finally, here was the validation I needed to continue. The daughter wanted to know if her grandfather was a peeping tom and spying on her. As her grandfather shook his head no, he explained to me how concerned he was for her and how important she was to him. He loves her and watches over her constantly, knowing and understanding everything that was happening in her life... even that she wears bikini underwear. As I relayed his message, both the daughter and Mom laughed and understood. This message began to change the daughter's life for the positive. So yes, the spirit world knows and sees everything and they do not miss a trick!

Healing a Past Life

I did a reading on a middle-aged woman who was feeling very stuck in her life. She experienced frustration with opening her psychic gifts and felt that she was just spinning her wheels, going nowhere.

I was guided to use two different types of decks, angel and fairy, and while laying out the cards, there were two that truly seemed special, as though they held the key or answer to this person's challenges.

The card on top was "Forgiveness," and the card directly underneath was "Power." As I laid my hands on these two cards, I had an instant flashback to one of her past lives. She had lived during the time of Atlantis and had misused her powers. The angels now came in and explained that since that lifetime, this woman never forgave herself, for she was part of a group that caused the destruction of Atlantis.

As I shared what the angels were showing me, she gasped and said, "Oh my God, I can't believe that you're saying this!" She experienced shivers throughout her whole body and from her emotional words and her physical reaction I knew the angels were strongly guiding me. We continued on with a forgiveness exercise to help heal the past.

I hope you enjoyed these angel readings and that they helped you to understand the process better.

PROGRAMMING YOUR CARDS FOR YES OR NO

Sometimes you need either a "Yes" or "No" answer to your question, but many card decks do not have these simple messages. Even if your card deck does have a "Yes" and "No" card, you will still need to program these particular cards for that response when working with the angels.

When programming your deck for "Yes" and "No," review each card in the deck and look for a card that looks or feels like a "Yes." Once you make your decision, write the name of the card down. This card represents your "Yes" response. Repeat the same process for "No" by fanning through your deck to see which card looks or feels like a "No" and write it down. If your deck already has a "Yes" and "No" card, know what they are and write them down.

You can change your yes/no cards any time, even with the decks that already contain yes/no cards.

Formulate your question first, then ask your question. While shuffling your cards and asking your question, make your intention known to the angels that you want a yes or no response using the cards that you programmed.

For example, I might want to ask a question about getting a new car. I formulate my question, already knowing my yes/no cards. After bringing in the angels, I shuffle the cards asking, "Is it for my highest good and the good of all concerned for me to buy a new car now? If the answer is yes, then show me the Michael card and if it is no, then show me the Gabriel card." Make sure you are clear about your yes/no cards, telling your angels what you are looking for. Repeat the question 2-3 times to make sure you are clear about your question and the angels are clear about what you are looking for.

Next, begin to pull cards any way you are guided to and trust. Your response will most likely pop up shortly in the deck. If you are three quarters of the way through your deck and neither card has appeared, it could mean you do not need to know or the decision is entirely up to you.

Remember, for each yes/no question you have, you will need to program your cards.

BLOCKS & PITFALLS

Have you ever received a reading that missed the mark or did not make sense? I have, and there are many reasons as to why this happens.

Here are a few major blockages and pitfalls that can happen, whether you are giving or receiving a reading.

- ♥ A person can block you because they really don't want a reading (they are not often consciously aware of this), but their friend may have pressured them into having a reading.

- ♥ Skeptics can influence your confidence. If you experience this, let them know you're not the right reader for them.

- ♥ Being too tired and fatigued.

♥   Having personal problems and difficulties.

♥   Experiencing self-doubt and anxiety.

♥   Being influenced by chemicals like alcohol, sugar, caffeine, nicotine and drugs.

♥   Having a full stomach may slow down your reading process.

♥   Sickness and depression.

♥   Being too preoccupied and distracted or too much mental clutter.

♥   Holding judgments, prejudices or hatred in your heart and mind.

If you experience any of these emotions or situations, you may want to either postpone the reading or refer them to another reader. If someone paid you already for their reading and the reading is not flowing, return their payment in full. Never be afraid or worry about what someone thinks. Honesty is the best policy and will yield you more business.

IN CLOSING

Learning to do angel readings can be a fun and easy way to connect and start a conversation with your angels. Angel readings can also be deeply moving, healing and even life altering.

Since there are many different spiritual beings in the angelic realm, it is quite useful to know who to call on for help and guidance. Always know that they are willing to assist at any time and await only your invitation to do so.

Taking Care of Self

In closing, self-care is essential to giving accurate and clear readings. Self-care is neither selfish nor self-indulgent. You cannot supply others from a dry well. You will find that if you take care of your own needs joyfully, your cup will overflow quite naturally and abundantly to all. When you support others from a place of fullness, you will feel renewed rather than depleted. Others will feel renewed too. We have something precious to give others when we have been nurturing and caring for ourselves and building up self-love. Always make time for you to indulge and practice "Spiritual Selfishness."

Enjoy your angel readings and may the angels light your way!

Elizabeth and the Angels

APPENDIX

It is vital to understand the function and purpose of the various archangels so you will know what it means if Archangel Michael or Archangel Gabriel shows up. Now let's discuss some of the more well known archangels and their specialties.

Archangel Ariel: **Angel of Nature**

Works with the elemental kingdom (nature and animals)

Environmental concerns and work

Careers involving animals or animal advocacy work

Helps to heal negative self-talk and self-sabotaging behavior

Assists with self-esteem and self-worth issues

Provides courage and strength to make changes in your life

Helps in creating abundance

Protection of environment (air, water and land)

Patron angel of animals and environment

Archangel Azrael: **Angel of Transition**

Assists souls transitioning into the spirit world

Helps with the grieving process

Guides grief counselors

Can connect you with deceased loved ones

Brings the message that you may be a medium

Carries messages from the spirit world

Comforts and brings healing energy to the grieving

Patron angel of clergy

Archangel Cassiel: **Angel of Temperance**

Offers healing energy to those who are feeling empty

Heals betrayal and abandonment issues

Tempers your mind and heart

Archangel Chamuel: **Angel of Harmony, Peace & Love**

Calms one's thoughts and mind chatter

Assists in search for a new job or change in career paths

Works toward global peace

Helps those in government positions involving peace negotiations

Mends damaged relationships

Heals ethnic and racial issues

Provides protection from lower energies and entities

Patron angel of peace

Archangel Gabriel: **Angel of Good News & Messages**

Assists with career change or transition

Provides guidance for starting a new business venture

Artists and creative projects

Entertainment

Radio and television careers

Music composers and singers

Writing, publishing and journalism

Creativity

Speaking your truth with love and compassion

School work

Teaching

Saying no and the right use of words

Fertility challenges

Helps expectant or want-to-be parents from conception to birth

Assists with child adoptions

Patron angel of all work in the area of communication

Archangel Haniel: **Angel of Grace**

Strengthens your psychic gifts

Assists with being open to receiving grace

Natural healing remedies and therapy

Helps to connect you with moon energy

Encourages feeling beautiful and seeing beauty

Defender of women issues

Archangel Jeremiel: **Angel of Prophecy**

Life review

Making life changes

Prophetic visions

Dreams and dream interpretation

Archangel Jophiel: **Angel of Illumination**

Exposes the truth in all situations

Self-realization

Discernment and wisdom

Absorbing information and studying

Increases awareness

Leads you towards inner peace

Provides support and guidance with legal issues

Archangel Metatron: **Highest of all the Archangels**

Balances your chakras with sacred geometry and Christ energy

Works with Mother Mary and children both here and in spirit

Guides the new children of Earth (Indigos and Crystals)

Children's issues

Walking on your spiritual path

Spiritual studies

Regulates the amount of light and energy we take in

Balances your energy

Works with sacred geometry

Alignment of energy

Patron angel of children

Archangel Michael: **Angel of Protection**

Boss of all Lightworkers

Oversees all the work of our guardian angels

Protection and shielding

Cuts and dissolves psychic etheric cords

Chakra clearing

Heals fear, anxiety and panic attacks

Holds life purpose path information and direction

Clears away blocks and obstacles

Space clearing (home and office)

Entity and demonic removal

Earthbound spirit releasement

Needing courage, will power or motivation

Taking back and reclaiming your personal power

Self-esteem and deserving issues

Strengthens your level of faith

Removes old vows

Mechanical and electrical problems

Patron angel of police and military personnel

Archangel Raguel: **Angel of Justice, Fairness & Harmony**

Resolving conflicts and arguments

Family harmony

Group work

Work involving mediation and conflict resolution

Divine order

Archangel Raphael: **Angel of Health & Healing**

You are a healer or need healing

Helps in locating a health professional

Oversees all forms of healing and helps healers of all kinds

Inspires, guides & supports healers (traditional and alternative)

Heals painful body parts

Caring for your physical body

Physical fitness and exercise

Eating right for your body

Weight loss

Oversees and directs medical care (people and animals)

Heals all forms of addictions and cravings

Inspires researchers in creating new medicines and procedures

Directs healers in developing new healing modalities

Protects travelers and their luggage

Archangel Raziel: **Angel of Magic & Alchemy**

Manifestation and alchemy

Understanding esoteric and
spiritual information

Helps to develop and strengthen
your psychic gifts

Legal issues

Archangel Sandalphon: **Angel of Music & Musings**

Creating or making music

Carries prayers to heaven

Answered prayers

Patron angel of music

Archangel Uriel: **Psychologist Angel**

Heals old heart wounds and
emotional distress

Assists in letting go of anger,
resentment and unforgiveness

Helps to locate a psychotherapist
or counselor

Guides counselors and the
therapy process

Heals past life karma

Helps with understanding another's view point

Protects and guides during natural disasters

Weather changes

Archangel Zadekiel: **Angel of Benevolence, Freedom & Mercy**

Compassion and being more compassionate

Forgiveness work

Brings in the energy of healing and transformation

Astell, Christine. *Discovering Angels*. London, England: Duncan Baird Publishers, 2005.

Bunson, Matthew. *Angels A to Z*. New York, NY: Three Rivers Press, 1996.

Choquette Ph.D., Sonia. *The Psychic Pathway*. New York, NY: Three Rivers Press, 1994.

Farmer Ph.D., Steven D. *Animal Spirit Guides*. Carlsbad, CA: Hay House, Inc., 2006.

Foley, Elizabeth J. *Awakening the Lightworker Within: A Personal Journey of Answering the Sacred Call*. Nashua, NH: Angel Street Publishing, LLC., 2008.

Guiley, Rosemary Ellen. *The Encyclopedia of Angels*. New York, NY: Checkmark Books, 2004.

Holland, John. *Psychic Navigator*. Carlsbad, CA: Hay House, Inc., 2004.

Lammey, William. *Karmic Tarot*. Franklin Lakes, NJ: New Page Books, 2002.

Pielmeier, Heidemarie, Schirner, Marcus. *Illustrated Tarot Spreads: 78 New Layouts for Personal Discovery*. New York, NY: Sterling Publishing Company, 1995.

Schneidere, Petra, Pieroth, Gerhard. *Archangels and Earthangels*. Twin Lakes, WI: Arcana Publishing, 2000.

Virtue, Doreen. *Archangels and Ascended Masters.* Carlsbad, CA: Hay House, Inc., 2003.

Virtue, Doreen. *Divine Guidance.* Los Angeles, CA: Renaissance Books, 1998.

Virtue, Doreen. *The Lightworker's Way.* Carlsbad, CA: Hay House, Inc., 1997.

ACKNOWLEDGEMENTS

To my amazing angelic support team, Archangel Michael, Archangel Gabriel, my guardian angels, the Ascended Masters and the many other spiritual beings that guide and support me in all ways.

I am deeply grateful to a very special friend and colleague, Allison. She gave me the perseverance to keep moving ahead and assisted with the editing of this book.

Many writing assistants came to my aid, so special thank yous to both Sharron King and Cathy Corcoran.

Most of all, thank you to the many students and angel clients throughout the years. You have been wonderful teachers for me and I am truly blessed by your presence in my life.

AUTHOR

Elizabeth J. Foley, EdM, MPH is an international Angelologist, teacher, healer, radio talk show host and author. She holds Master degrees in Counseling and Guidance and in Public Health. She is a doctoral candidate in Metaphysics at the American Institute of Holistic Theology and has appeared on various radio and television shows including the Liz Walker Show - WBZ 4 - Boston. Elizabeth conducts private angel sessions and facilitates unique spiritual workshops on angels, psychic development and Soul Therapy© throughout the country. She makes her home in Nashua, NH. For more information, please visit www.divinehealing.us.

ANGEL HEALING PRACTITIONER©
CERTIFICATION PROGRAM

The Angel Healing Practitioner© certification course encourages you to awaken your intuition, read energy, conduct angel readings confidently and to learn and practice angel healing techniques. You will also discover the ways in which the angelic realm communicates with you and learn to receive messages, information and Divine guidance and healing from the angels.

The main objective of the course is to:

♥ Teach you how to give accurate and healing angel readings, explore various card spreads and how to interpret the meaning.

♥ Help you discover your natural Divine communication style and how to combine clairvoyance, clairaudience, clairsentience and claircognizance with your card readings to gain deeper insight and understanding of your angels' messages.

♥ Learn about the angelic realm including information about guardian angels, archangels, Ascended Masters, fairies and deceased loved ones.

♥ Teach you how to prepare yourself and your cards for conducting an angel reading.

♥ Practice automatic writing with the angels for receiving messages and information.

♥ Learn and practice angel healing techniques for self and others.

♥ Become familiar with the practical and ethical considerations involved in becoming an Angel Healing Practitioner©.

♥ Learn techniques to build your practice.

For more information and dates, please contact Elizabeth J. Foley at Divine Healing, P.O. Box 7124, Nashua, NH 03060 or visit www.divinehealing.us.

SOUL THERAPY PRACTITIONER©
CERTIFICATION PROGRAM

Each of us has a unique Divine soul and soul mission and the Soul Therapy Practitioner© (STP) Program is dedicated to an in-depth discovery, healing and clearing of the different aspects of your mental, emotional, physical and spiritual bodies. The goal of the STP program is to help you discover and align your inner spiritual life with your outer life and to empower yourself and others. In this powerful certification course, not only will you embark on your own inner sacred quest, but you also will learn how to assist others on their spiritual journey and discovery. This program is limited to eight people only and attendance is required for all four weekends.

The Soul Therapy Practitioner© program is a four-weekend self-guided program that includes:

- ♥ What is the Soul and Understanding the Energy of Your Soul

- ♥ Listening and Connecting to Your Soul

- ♥ Understanding and Opening the Seven Seals (spiritual issues and the chakras)

- ♥ The Seven Rays and How They Guide Your Soul

- ♥ Development of the Soul (discovering your soul age, level and role)

- ♥ Basics of Spiritual Psychology (exploring the twelve life lessons & creating a spiritual psychological profile)

- ♥ Awakening and Clearing the Physical, Mental, Emotional and Spiritual Body

- ♥ Tools for Emotional and Spiritual Healing

- ♥ Tests of Initiation of the Soul

- ♥ Steps to Attain Mastery and Manifest Your Mission

For more information and dates, please contact Elizabeth J. Foley at Divine Healing, P.O. Box 7124, Nashua, NH 03060 or visit www.divinehealing.us.

ANGEL STREET PUBLISHING, LLC

OTHER TITLES BY AUTHOR

BOOKS

Awakening the Lightworker Within:
A Personal Journey of Answering the Sacred Call

CARD DECKS

Nature Spirits Oracle Cards

CDs

Meditations for Healing and Spiritual Transformation
with Elizabeth Foley